The Power of Effective Interviews

for Employers and Employees

By Dr. Raul Dominguez

The Power of Effective Interviews for Employers and Employees

Copyright © 2023 Raul Dominguez
All rights reserved.
ISBN:9798852698100

Raul Dominguez
Miami FL, USA

Effective interviews have the power to transform by enabling employers to uncover hidden talents and candidates to showcase their true capabilities. This leads to the forging of meaningful connections that shape the future of organizations and individuals.

Dr. R. Dominguez

Content

Abstract:

"The Power of Effective Interviews for Employers and Employees" is a comprehensive guide that unlocks the key to successful talent acquisition and optimal workplace dynamics. Authored by Dr. Raul Dominguez, a distinguished expert in Industrial-Organizational (IO) Psychology, this book delves into the intricacies of the interview process, offering a wealth of insights and practical strategies for both employers and candidates.

In this book, employers gain invaluable tools to conduct interviews that go beyond the surface, tapping into candidates' true potential and identifying the perfect fit for their organization. From crafting purposeful interview questions to fostering a positive candidate experience, employers learn how to create an inclusive and engaging interview environment that yields exceptional results.

For candidates, "The Power of Effective Interviews" provides a roadmap to showcase their skills and achievements authentically. Readers discover how to navigate challenging interview scenarios, present themselves confidently, and effectively communicate their unique value to potential employers.

Dr. Dominguez draws from his vast experience and research to address diverse topics, including the significance of feedback in the interview process, the role of technology in modern interviews, and the impact of organizational culture on talent acquisition.

With additional resources for further learning and thought-provoking insights, this book serves as an indispensable tool for HR professionals, hiring managers, job seekers, and anyone seeking to unlock the full potential of effective interviews in shaping thriving workplaces and fostering career growth.

"The Power of Effective Interviews for Employers and Employees" is a powerful exploration of the interview process, illuminating the transformative impact it holds in fostering meaningful connections and driving success in the ever-evolving world of work.

Chapter 1: Introduction

1.1 Overview of the Book

Welcome to "The Power of Effective Interviews for Employers and Employees." This book is a comprehensive guide that aims to equip both employers and job seekers with the necessary knowledge and skills to excel in the interview process. Interviews play a pivotal role in the employment journey, serving as a critical tool for employers to assess candidates and for applicants to showcase their qualifications and suitability for a position.

Throughout this book, we will explore various aspects of interviews, including the different types of interviews, the interview process, effective interview techniques, strategies for success, and the importance of fairness and inclusivity. By delving into these topics, you will gain valuable insights and practical tips to make the most out of every interview opportunity.

1.2 Importance of Effective Interviews

Interviews hold significant weight in the hiring process, as they provide a platform for employers to evaluate candidates beyond what is presented on paper. For employers, conducting effective interviews allows them to assess the skills, qualifications, and potential cultural fit of applicants, ultimately aiding in making informed hiring decisions.

On the other hand, interviews are crucial for job seekers, offering them the chance to articulate their experiences, demonstrate their abilities, and leave a lasting impression on potential employers. A well-executed interview can be the gateway to securing the desired job and advancing one's career.

Understanding the power of interviews and harnessing the necessary skills to navigate them successfully can be a game-changer for both employers and employees. Employers can significantly enhance their recruitment processes by identifying the most suitable candidates, while job seekers can leverage interviews to showcase their strengths and stand out from the competition.

In this book, we will delve into the intricacies of effective interviews, exploring the techniques and strategies that can help employers conduct insightful and fair assessments, as well as providing job seekers with the tools to prepare thoroughly, present themselves confidently, and make a lasting impact on their interviewers.

By mastering the art of interviews, employers can attract and select top talent, contributing to the success and growth of their organizations. Employees, on the other hand, can secure the job opportunities they desire, paving the way for personal and professional fulfillment.

Throughout the following chapters, we will explore the interview process from both perspectives, guiding employers on how to conduct interviews that yield valuable insights, and empowering employees with the knowledge and skills to excel in their interviews.

In the upcoming chapters, we will discuss the different types of interviews, the preparation necessary for successful interviews, and the techniques to establish rapport and engage candidates effectively. We will also explore how to evaluate candidate competencies, manage challenging interview situations, and navigate salary negotiations. Moreover, we will highlight the importance of fair and inclusive interviews and the role of technology in the modern interview landscape.

So, whether you are an employer looking to refine your interviewing techniques or a job seeker eager to leave a lasting impression, this book will serve as your comprehensive guide to unlocking the power of effective interviews. Let's embark on this journey together and uncover the secrets to interview success.

Chapter 2: Understanding the Interview Process

In this chapter, we will delve into the intricacies of the interview process, which forms the foundation for successful interactions between employers and job seekers. Understanding the different types of interviews, how to prepare for them, and the logistics involved are essential for both employers and employees to make the most out of this critical stage in the employment journey.

2.1 Types of Interviews

Before diving into the interview process, it's crucial to grasp the various types of interviews that employers may use to evaluate candidates. Each type has its unique approach, and understanding these differences can help employers select the most suitable format for their specific hiring needs.

2.1.1 Structured Interviews

Structured interviews are standardized, consistent, and objective in nature. In this type of interview, all candidates are asked the same set of predetermined questions. The questions are carefully designed to assess specific job-related competencies and skills. Structured interviews allow for easier comparison between candidates as they are all evaluated based on the same criteria.

The key advantage of structured interviews is their reliability and validity, as they minimize biases and ensure that candidates are assessed fairly. Employers can analyze the responses consistently and make more informed hiring decisions.

2.1.2 Unstructured Interviews

Unstructured interviews, in contrast, are more informal and flexible. In these interviews, the questions are not standardized, and the flow of the conversation may vary based on the candidate's responses. While this approach allows for a more personalized interaction, it can also introduce bias, as different candidates may be asked different questions or evaluated on different criteria.

Employers who opt for unstructured interviews should be cautious of potential biases and should strive to focus on relevant job-related qualities during the conversation.

2.1.3 Behavioral Interviews

Behavioral interviews focus on past behaviors and experiences as indicators of future performance. In this type of interview, candidates are asked to provide specific examples of how they handled certain situations in the past. Employers are interested in understanding how candidates acted in real-life scenarios, as this can offer valuable insights into their problem-solving abilities, decision-making skills, and interpersonal competencies.

The STAR method (Situation, Task, Action, Result) is commonly used in behavioral interviews to structure the candidate's responses effectively.

2.1.4 Panel Interviews

Panel interviews involve multiple interviewers, typically from different departments or roles within the organization. This format allows for a more comprehensive assessment of the candidate, as different panel members can bring diverse perspectives and expertise to the evaluation process.

While panel interviews can be intimidating for candidates, they provide a more holistic view of the applicant's qualifications and cultural fit within the organization.

2.2 Preparing for Interviews

A well-prepared interview is essential for both employers and employees. Employers must lay the groundwork for an effective interview process, while job seekers need to thoroughly prepare themselves to make a positive impression. Let's explore the key aspects of interview preparation.

2.2.1 Defining Job Requirements

Before initiating the interview process, employers should have a clear understanding of the job requirements and the specific skills and competencies needed for the role. This clarity will guide the development of relevant interview questions and evaluation criteria.

By having a well-defined job description, employers can ensure that the interview process is focused on identifying candidates who possess the necessary qualifications to excel in the position.

2.2.2 Creating Interview Criteria

Building on the job requirements, employers should establish interview criteria that align with the organization's values and goals. These criteria will serve as benchmarks for evaluating candidates and making hiring decisions based on merit.

Interview criteria may include technical skills, soft skills, cultural fit, adaptability, and any other attributes crucial for success in the role and within the organization.

2.2.3 Developing Interview Questions

Once the job requirements and interview criteria are set, employers can proceed to develop interview questions that effectively assess candidates' qualifications. The questions should be designed to elicit comprehensive responses, allowing employers to evaluate how well candidates meet the established criteria.

In structured interviews, the questions should remain consistent for all candidates to facilitate fair comparisons. For behavioral interviews, questions should prompt candidates to share real-life experiences that demonstrate their abilities and problem-solving skills.

The questions should be thoughtfully crafted to avoid biases and discriminatory practices, focusing solely on the candidates' qualifications and suitability for the job.

2.3 Interview Logistics

The logistics of the interview process are vital to ensuring a smooth and efficient experience for both employers and candidates. Failing to address logistical considerations can lead to confusion and may reflect poorly on the organization.

2.3.1 Scheduling Interviews

Employers should promptly schedule interviews once they have received applications from potential candidates. Timely communication reflects professionalism and respect for the candidates' time.

The scheduling process should also involve coordinating availability among the interviewers, particularly in panel interviews, to ensure all key stakeholders can participate.

2.3.2 Setting Up the Interview Space

Whether the interviews are conducted in person or virtually, creating an appropriate interview environment is crucial. In-person interviews should be held in a quiet and private setting, free from distractions. Virtual interviews should leverage reliable video conferencing tools, and candidates should be provided with clear instructions on how to join the virtual meeting.

A well-prepared and organized interview space sets a positive tone for the interaction and allows both employers and candidates to focus on the conversation.

2.3.3 Interviewer Training

Interviewer training is often overlooked but is critical for conducting effective interviews. Interviewers should be familiar with the interview process, the interview questions, and the evaluation criteria.

Training should also address potential biases and ensure that interviewers are equipped to assess candidates fairly and objectively. Interviewer training can significantly enhance the quality and consistency of the interview process across the organization.

In conclusion, understanding the different types of interviews and preparing effectively for the interview process is fundamental to successful interactions between employers and job seekers. Employers must carefully design interview formats that align with their hiring objectives, while candidates should invest time and effort in thoroughly preparing for each interview opportunity.

In the next chapter, we will delve deeper into the techniques that employers can employ to establish rapport and engage candidates effectively during the interview, setting the stage for a productive and insightful conversation. Similarly, job seekers will learn how to present themselves confidently and leave a lasting impression on their interviewers. Let's proceed on this journey to unlock the power of effective interviews together.

Chapter 3: Mastering Interview Techniques for Employers

In Chapter 3, we will explore the essential interview techniques that employers can utilize to conduct insightful and effective interviews. The interview process is not merely a one-sided evaluation of candidates; it is an opportunity for employers to engage with potential employees, understand their capabilities, and assess their fit within the organization. Employers who master these techniques can attract top talent and make well-informed hiring decisions that contribute to the overall success of their company.

3.1 Establishing Rapport and Engaging Candidates

Building a positive and comfortable rapport with candidates is crucial for creating an environment where they can showcase their true potential. When candidates feel at ease during the interview, they are more likely to provide honest and genuine responses, giving employers a more accurate assessment of their qualifications and personalities. Here are some techniques to establish rapport and engage candidates effectively:

3.1.1 Nonverbal Communication

Employers should be mindful of their nonverbal cues during interviews. Maintaining good eye contact, offering a warm and friendly smile, and using open body language can help candidates feel welcome and valued. Conversely, negative or disinterested nonverbal cues can make candidates feel uneasy or discouraged.

Active listening is also essential in demonstrating engagement. Nodding, providing verbal cues, and taking notes when appropriate show candidates that their responses are being heard and considered thoughtfully.

3.1.2 Asking Open-Ended Questions

To encourage candidates to share more about themselves and their experiences, employers should ask open-ended questions. Open-ended questions prompt candidates to provide detailed responses, offering deeper insights into their thought processes and problem-solving abilities.

For example, instead of asking a simple "yes" or "no" question like, "Do you have experience in project management?" employers could ask, "Can you tell us about a project you managed in your previous role? What challenges did you face, and how did you overcome them?"

Open-ended questions invite candidates to elaborate on their experiences and demonstrate their competencies in a more comprehensive manner.

3.2 Conducting Effective Behavioral Interviews

Behavioral interviews are powerful tools for employers to assess how candidates have handled specific situations in the past and predict their future performance. Conducting behavioral interviews effectively involves using structured questions and probing for detailed responses. Here's how employers can master this technique:

3.2.1 Using the STAR Method

The STAR method is an effective framework for structuring behavioral interview questions and evaluating candidate responses. STAR stands for Situation, Task, Action, and Result.

Employers should ask candidates to describe a specific Situation or context, the Task or challenge they faced, the Action they took to address the situation, and the Result or outcome of their actions. This format allows for a clear and comprehensive understanding of the candidate's experiences and how they approach problem-solving.

For instance, an employer might ask, "Can you share a time when you had to handle a difficult customer complaint? What steps did you take to address their concerns, and what was the outcome?"

3.2.2 Probing for Details

To gain deeper insights into candidates' past experiences, employers should follow up on their initial responses with probing questions. Probing questions seek more specific information about the candidate's actions, thought processes, and outcomes.

For example, after hearing a candidate's response to the customer complaint scenario, an employer might follow up with, "How did you remain calm and composed during the interaction? What strategies did you use to de-escalate the situation?"

Probing for details allows employers to understand the candidate's decision-making process and the effectiveness of their actions in various situations.

3.3 Evaluating Candidate Competencies

Evaluating candidate competencies is a critical aspect of the interview process. Employers must assess not only the candidate's technical skills but also their soft skills and cultural fit within the organization. Here are some techniques to effectively evaluate candidate competencies:

3.3.1 Assessing Skills and Qualifications

To assess technical skills and qualifications, employers should tailor interview questions to specific job requirements. Asking candidates about their experience with relevant tools, software, or processes can provide valuable insights into their abilities.

Additionally, conducting skills assessments or work simulations can further validate candidates' competencies and ensure they can perform the tasks required for the role.

3.3.2 Evaluating Cultural Fit

Cultural fit is essential for successful long-term employment. During the interview, employers can assess cultural fit by asking questions related to the organization's values, mission, and work environment.

For example, employers might ask, "Our company values collaboration and teamwork. Can you share an experience where you collaborated with colleagues to achieve a common goal?"

By evaluating cultural fit, employers can identify candidates who align with the company's values and are likely to thrive in its work culture.

In conclusion, mastering interview techniques is fundamental for employers to conduct effective interviews and make informed hiring decisions. Building rapport and engaging candidates, utilizing behavioral interviews, and evaluating competencies are key elements in this process. Employers who adopt these techniques will be better equipped to attract top talent and build a strong and dynamic workforce.

In the next chapter, we will shift our focus to job seekers, exploring how they can excel in their interviews by preparing thoroughly, presenting themselves confidently, and effectively showcasing their skills and accomplishments. Let's continue this journey to unlock the power of effective interviews for both employers and employees.

Chapter 4: Excelling in Job Interviews for Employees

In Chapter 4, we will delve into the strategies and techniques that job seekers can employ to excel in their job interviews. A well-prepared and confident approach can significantly impact the interview's outcome, increase the chances of securing the desired position, and set the foundation for a successful career path. Let's explore how job seekers can effectively navigate the interview process.

4.1 Preparing for the Interview

Proper preparation is the cornerstone of interview success. Thoroughly researching the company, understanding the job requirements, and practicing responses to common interview questions are essential steps in preparing for an interview.

4.1.1 Researching the Company

Before attending an interview, candidates should conduct comprehensive research on the company they are applying to. This involves understanding the company's mission, values, products, services, and recent achievements. Familiarity with the company's history and culture demonstrates genuine interest and enthusiasm, which can impress the interviewer.

For example, if a candidate is applying to a tech startup, they might research the company's recent product launches, its impact on the industry, and any innovative projects or initiatives that align with their own skills and interests. This information can be found on the company's website, press releases, and reputable news sources.

4.1.2 Reviewing Common Interview Questions

Candidates should anticipate and practice responses to common interview questions. These questions often revolve around strengths and weaknesses, previous work experiences, problem-solving abilities, and career aspirations. Preparing thoughtful and concise answers to these questions can help candidates articulate their qualifications effectively.

For instance, a candidate may practice answering the question, "What is your greatest strength?" by highlighting a specific skill or quality relevant to the job, such as strong analytical abilities backed by examples from previous projects.

4.1.3 Practicing Interview Responses

Mock interviews with a friend or career coach can be immensely beneficial. Practicing responses to anticipated questions allows candidates to refine their answers, gain confidence in their communication skills, and receive constructive feedback.

Through practice, candidates can improve their delivery, avoid rambling or excessive jargon, and ensure that they present their experiences and accomplishments in a clear and compelling manner.

4.2 Presenting Yourself Confidently

Confidence is key to making a positive impression during the interview. Candidates can project confidence through their demeanor, appearance, and communication style.

4.2.1 Dressing Professionally

Dressing appropriately for the interview demonstrates professionalism and respect for the company's culture. Candidates should research the company's dress code and choose an outfit that aligns with the company's norms.

For example, if the company has a business casual dress code, candidates might wear neatly pressed slacks or a skirt with a collared shirt or blouse. In contrast, if the company has a more formal dress code, candidates may opt for a tailored suit and tie or an appropriate business dress.

4.2.2 Demonstrating Positive Body Language

Body language is a crucial aspect of nonverbal communication. Candidates should maintain good posture, make eye contact, and offer a firm handshake when greeting the interviewer.

Throughout the interview, candidates should avoid fidgeting, crossing their arms (which may be perceived as defensive), or slouching (which may convey disinterest). Instead, candidates should project openness and engagement through attentive and positive body language.

4.3 Highlighting Your Skills and Accomplishments

Effectively showcasing skills and accomplishments can differentiate candidates from others with similar qualifications. Candidates should use specific examples from their work experiences to demonstrate their value and potential contribution to the company.

4.3.1 Crafting a Compelling Resume

A well-crafted resume serves as a foundation for interview discussions. Candidates should tailor their resumes to highlight their most relevant skills and achievements for the specific job they are applying for.

For example, if a candidate is applying for a marketing position, their resume should emphasize marketing-related experiences, such as successful campaigns, social media strategies, or lead generation efforts.

4.3.2 Developing Your Personal Brand

Candidates can stand out by developing a strong personal brand that aligns with their career goals. This includes identifying their unique strengths, skills, and values and communicating them consistently throughout the interview.

For instance, a candidate interested in project management might emphasize their ability to efficiently organize and lead teams, demonstrating a track record of successful project completions.

4.4 Answering Interview Questions Effectively

During the interview, candidates should strive to answer questions thoughtfully and confidently. Providing specific examples and relevant experiences helps interviewers assess a candidate's qualifications more effectively.

4.4.1 Providing Specific Examples

When asked behavioral or situational questions, candidates should use the STAR method (Situation, Task, Action, Result) to structure their responses.

For instance, if asked to describe a time when they encountered a challenging situation at work, candidates might respond with:

"During my previous role as a project manager, we faced a tight deadline to deliver a critical client project. The team was overwhelmed, and tensions were rising. To address the situation, I organized a brief team meeting to reevaluate priorities and reallocate resources. We also implemented daily progress check-ins to ensure everyone was on track. As a result of these actions, we not only met the deadline but also received positive feedback from the client for our efficiency and teamwork."

4.4.2 Demonstrating Problem-Solving Abilities

Candidates should be prepared to discuss how they approach problem-solving. This may involve explaining their decision-making process, analytical skills, and ability to adapt to unexpected challenges.

For example, a candidate might share:

"When confronted with a complex problem, I believe in thoroughly analyzing the situation, gathering relevant data, and considering various perspectives. In my previous role, we encountered a significant budget cut midway through a project. I assembled a cross-functional team to brainstorm cost-saving measures while maintaining the project's quality. By leveraging our collective expertise, we were able to identify alternative suppliers and negotiate better deals, allowing us to complete the project within the new budget constraints."

By providing specific and detailed responses, candidates demonstrate their abilities in a tangible and impactful manner.

In conclusion, excelling in job interviews requires thorough preparation, confident presentation, and effective communication of skills and accomplishments. Candidates who invest time and effort into preparing for interviews increase their chances of leaving a lasting and positive impression on employers.

In the next chapter, we will shift our focus to employers, exploring the techniques they can use to effectively assess candidate competencies, manage challenging interview situations, and ensure a fair and inclusive interview process. Let's continue on this journey to unlock the power of effective interviews for both employers and employees.

Chapter 5: Ensuring a Fair and Inclusive Interview Process

In Chapter 5, we will delve into the importance of conducting fair and inclusive interviews. A fair and inclusive interview process is not only ethically sound but also crucial for attracting diverse talent and promoting a positive company culture. By adopting inclusive practices, employers can create an environment that fosters innovation, creativity, and collaboration. Let's explore the strategies and techniques to ensure a fair and inclusive interview process.

5.1 Promoting Diversity and Inclusion

Promoting diversity and inclusion should be a central focus for employers during the interview process. A diverse workforce brings together individuals with varied backgrounds, perspectives, and experiences, leading to a richer and more innovative work environment.

5.1.1 Creating Inclusive Job Descriptions

The first step in promoting diversity and inclusion is crafting inclusive job descriptions. Employers should use gender-neutral language and avoid any terms or requirements that might inadvertently discourage certain groups from applying.

For example, instead of using words like "aggressive" or "dominant," employers can use language that emphasizes collaboration and teamwork.

Inclusive job descriptions are more likely to attract a diverse pool of applicants, giving employers a broader range of candidates to consider.

5.1.2 Eliminating Bias in Interview Questions

Employers must be mindful of bias when developing interview questions. Bias can manifest in both the content of the questions and how they are asked.

To eliminate bias, employers should ensure that interview questions are relevant to the job requirements and do not favor any particular demographic. Additionally, questions should be phrased in a way that does not assume gender, race, or other characteristics of the candidate.

Conducting a review of interview questions with a focus on bias awareness can help employers identify and rectify any potentially problematic questions.

5.2 Implementing Structured Interview Techniques

To maintain fairness and consistency throughout the interview process, employers can adopt structured interview techniques.

5.2.1 Standardizing Interview Processes

In structured interviews, all candidates are asked the same set of predetermined questions. By standardizing the interview process, employers can compare candidates more objectively based on the same criteria.

This approach minimizes bias and ensures that candidates are evaluated solely on their qualifications and responses, rather than subjective factors.

5.2.2 Using Evaluation Rubrics

Employers can use evaluation rubrics to assess candidate responses consistently. An evaluation rubric outlines specific criteria and corresponding rating scales for each question.

For example, a rubric may include criteria such as "clarity of response," "relevant examples provided," and "ability to handle challenging questions." Interviewers can use the rubric to rate each candidate's performance objectively.

Using evaluation rubrics adds structure and transparency to the evaluation process, making it easier for employers to make informed hiring decisions.

5.3 Conducting Ethical Interviews

Ethics play a crucial role in the interview process. Employers must ensure that all candidates are treated respectfully and that their privacy and confidentiality are upheld.

5.3.1 Respecting Candidate Privacy

Employers should only ask questions that are directly relevant to the job requirements and avoid probing into personal matters that are unrelated to the role.

For instance, employers should refrain from asking about a candidate's marital status, family plans, or health conditions, as such inquiries are invasive and potentially discriminatory.

5.3.2 Maintaining Confidentiality

During the interview, candidates may share sensitive information about their current employer, colleagues, or clients. Employers must assure candidates that any information disclosed during the interview will be treated with strict confidentiality.

Interviewers should avoid sharing confidential candidate information with individuals who are not directly involved in the hiring process. This commitment to confidentiality fosters trust between the candidate and the employer.

5.4 Leveraging Technology for Inclusive Interviews

Technology can play a significant role in promoting inclusivity and accessibility during the interview process.

5.4.1 Utilizing Video Interviews

Video interviews offer a flexible and inclusive approach, particularly for candidates who may face geographical or scheduling challenges. Video interviews enable employers to engage with candidates regardless of their physical location, making the interview process more accessible.

Employers should ensure that the video interview platform they use is user-friendly and compatible with various devices and internet connections.

5.4.2 AI and Automation in Interviews

While leveraging AI and automation in interviews can enhance efficiency and standardization, employers must be cautious about potential biases embedded in AI algorithms.

AI tools used for candidate screening or evaluation should be thoroughly tested and regularly audited to ensure they do not perpetuate discriminatory practices.

In conclusion, ensuring a fair and inclusive interview process is essential for attracting diverse talent, promoting a positive company culture, and fostering innovation. By promoting diversity, eliminating bias, implementing structured interview techniques, and utilizing technology inclusively and ethically, employers can create a welcoming environment that encourages all candidates to bring their unique perspectives and skills to the table.

In the next chapter, we will explore the post-interview steps and decision-making process for employers. We will discuss how to assess and compare candidates, conduct reference checks, extend job offers, and facilitate a smooth onboarding process. Let's continue on this journey to unlock the power of effective interviews for both employers and employees.

Chapter 6: Post-Interview Steps and Decision Making

In Chapter 6, we will shift our focus to the post-interview steps and the decision-making process for employers. The interview is just one part of the hiring journey, and what happens after the interviews are conducted plays a significant role in finalizing the hiring decisions and ensuring a successful onboarding process for the selected candidates. Let's explore the crucial steps employers should take in the post-interview phase.

6.1 Assessing and Comparing Candidates

After conducting interviews, employers must assess and compare the performance of each candidate to make an informed hiring decision. This step involves evaluating the candidates' qualifications, interview responses, and overall fit with the company culture and requirements of the position.

6.1.1 Reviewing Interview Notes and Feedback

Interviewers should review the notes and feedback collected during each candidate's interview. This may include written notes, evaluation rubrics, or any assessments conducted during the interview process.

Reviewing interview notes helps interviewers refresh their memory about each candidate's performance and enables them to objectively evaluate each candidate's strengths and areas for improvement.

6.1.2 Conducting Reference Checks

Reference checks are an essential part of the assessment process. Contacting a candidate's previous employers, supervisors, or colleagues can provide valuable insights into the candidate's work ethic, performance, and interpersonal skills.

When conducting reference checks, employers should ask open-ended questions to encourage honest and detailed responses. Questions could focus on the candidate's work style, problem-solving abilities, and interactions with others.

Reference checks should complement the information obtained during the interview, helping employers confirm the accuracy of the candidate's claims and evaluate their suitability for the role.

6.2 Extending Job Offers and Onboarding

Once the assessment process is complete, employers can extend job offers to the selected candidates. The job offer should be clear, concise, and include all relevant details about the position, such as salary, benefits, starting date, and other essential information.

6.2.1 Making an Offer

When making a job offer, employers should communicate the offer in a personalized and positive manner. Emphasize the candidate's strengths and the unique contributions they will bring to the organization.

It is essential to give candidates sufficient time to consider the offer and make an informed decision. Promptly answering any questions or concerns the candidate may have demonstrates professionalism and a commitment to open communication.

6.2.2 Assisting with Transition and Integration

After a candidate accepts the job offer, employers should focus on facilitating a smooth onboarding process. Onboarding includes helping the new employee transition into their role, familiarizing them with company policies and procedures, and providing necessary training and resources.

A well-structured onboarding process ensures that the new employee feels welcomed and supported, increasing the likelihood of long-term engagement and success within the organization.

6.3 Handling Unsuccessful Candidates

It is essential to treat all candidates with respect and courtesy, including those who were not selected for the position. Employers should communicate the outcome of the selection process promptly and professionally.

6.3.1 Providing Feedback

Offering constructive feedback to unsuccessful candidates can be beneficial to their professional growth and development. While it may not be feasible to provide detailed feedback to every candidate, employers can offer general insights on areas for improvement.

For example, employers might say, "While we were impressed with your experience in marketing, we ultimately selected a candidate who had more direct experience with our target audience."

Feedback can help candidates understand where they can enhance their skills and qualifications for future opportunities.

6.3.2 Encouraging Future Consideration

Employers should encourage candidates to consider future openings within the company and express appreciation for their interest in the organization.

Building a positive candidate experience, even for those who were not selected, can leave a lasting impression on candidates and strengthen the company's employer brand.

In conclusion, the post-interview steps and decision-making process are integral to hiring the right candidates and ensuring a successful onboarding experience. Assessing and comparing candidates, conducting reference checks, extending job offers, and handling unsuccessful candidates professionally contribute to an effective and inclusive hiring process.

In the next chapter, we will explore the role of technology in the interview process, including video interviews, AI tools for screening, and ethical considerations surrounding the use of technology. Let's continue on this journey to unlock the power of effective interviews for both employers and employees.

Chapter 7: Technology in the Interview Process

In Chapter 7, we will explore the impact of technology on the interview process, including the use of video interviews, AI tools for candidate screening, and ethical considerations related to technology integration. Embracing technology can enhance efficiency, broaden access to candidates, and provide valuable insights into the hiring process. However, it is crucial to strike a balance between leveraging technology and preserving the human touch in the interview experience.

7.1 Video Interviews: Broadening Access and Flexibility

Video interviews have become increasingly popular as organizations seek to streamline their interview process and expand their talent pool. Video interviews allow employers to engage with candidates remotely, irrespective of geographical locations, reducing time and travel costs.

Furthermore, video interviews offer greater flexibility to both employers and candidates. Employers can schedule interviews at convenient times, accommodating candidates from different time zones or with busy schedules. Candidates, on the other hand, can participate in interviews from the comfort of their own environment, reducing interview-related stress and facilitating a more authentic conversation.

For example, a multinational company with offices in various countries can conduct initial video interviews to shortlist candidates for further rounds. This approach saves time and resources compared to flying candidates from different regions for in-person interviews.

7.2 AI Tools for Candidate Screening: Efficiency and Data-Driven Decisions

AI-powered tools for candidate screening have gained traction in recent years. These tools use algorithms to analyze large volumes of applicant data and identify potential matches for specific roles. AI can efficiently review resumes, assess qualifications, and identify patterns that align with the organization's hiring criteria.

AI tools can be particularly valuable in high-volume recruitment situations, where manually reviewing thousands of applications can be time-consuming and overwhelming.

However, while AI can streamline the screening process, it is essential to ensure that the algorithms used are free from biases. Biases in AI algorithms can perpetuate discrimination and hinder diversity and inclusion efforts. It is crucial for organizations to regularly audit and test their AI tools to minimize bias and ensure fair candidate evaluations.

For instance, an e-commerce company seeking customer support representatives may use AI-powered software to analyze candidates' resumes for relevant experience, communication skills, and customer service-related keywords. This initial screening narrows down the candidate pool, allowing recruiters to focus on the most promising applicants.

7.3 Ethical Considerations with Technology in Interviews

While technology offers numerous benefits to the interview process, it also raises ethical considerations that employers must address. Ensuring data privacy, maintaining candidate confidentiality, and minimizing biases are essential aspects of ethical technology integration.

7.3.1 Data Privacy and Candidate Consent

Employers must be transparent about how candidate data will be used and stored during the interview process. Candidates should be informed about data retention policies and their rights regarding their personal information.

Obtaining explicit consent from candidates before using AI tools or recording video interviews is critical to respecting candidates' privacy.

7.3.2 Mitigating Bias in AI Algorithms

As mentioned earlier, bias in AI algorithms can have detrimental effects on candidate evaluations. Employers must actively monitor and address biases in AI systems to ensure fair and equitable hiring practices.

This may involve working with data scientists and diversity experts to develop and validate algorithms that consider a diverse range of candidate backgrounds and experiences.

For example, an AI algorithm used for resume screening should be trained on a diverse dataset that represents various demographics and backgrounds, thus reducing the risk of inherent biases.

In conclusion, technology has significantly transformed the interview process, offering advantages such as accessibility, efficiency, and data-driven decision-making. Employers can leverage video interviews and AI-powered tools to streamline candidate evaluations and enhance the overall recruitment experience. However, it is essential to uphold ethical standards, ensuring privacy, and mitigating biases to maintain fairness and inclusivity throughout the hiring journey.

In the next chapter, we will explore how employers can navigate challenging interview scenarios and handle difficult situations with professionalism and tact. Let's continue on this journey to unlock the power of effective interviews for both employers and employees.

Chapter 8: Navigating Challenging Interview Scenarios with Professionalism

In Chapter 8, we will explore how employers can navigate challenging interview scenarios with professionalism and tact. Interviews can present unexpected situations that require careful handling to ensure a positive candidate experience and a fair assessment of candidates' qualifications. By preparing for these scenarios and responding thoughtfully, employers can create a welcoming and respectful environment that reflects well on the organization. Let's delve into some common challenging interview scenarios and how to address them.

8.1 Addressing Gaps in Employment

When interviewing candidates, employers may encounter gaps in their employment history. These gaps could result from personal reasons, career transitions, or other life circumstances. Addressing employment gaps with sensitivity and understanding is crucial to avoid making candidates uncomfortable or discouraged.

8.1.1 Focus on Skills and Achievements

During the interview, employers should focus on the candidate's skills, qualifications, and achievements rather than fixating on employment gaps. Discussing the candidate's accomplishments and how they align with the job requirements can provide valuable insights into their suitability for the position.

For example, if a candidate has a gap due to taking time off to care for a family member, the employer might say, "I see that during your previous role, you successfully led a team and implemented a new process that improved efficiency. Can you tell us more about your experience in handling such projects?"

By concentrating on the candidate's abilities and accomplishments, employers can create a positive interview experience that allows candidates to showcase their strengths.

8.1.2 Frame Questions Positively

If an employer needs to inquire about an employment gap, they should frame the question positively and with empathy. Avoid assumptions and potential biases while seeking a better understanding of the candidate's career journey.

Instead of asking, "Why do you have a gap in your employment history?" employers can ask, "I noticed there is a gap in your employment history during these years. Can you share with us any experiences or projects you pursued during that time?"

By using a compassionate approach, employers demonstrate understanding and respect for the candidate's circumstances.

8.2 Handling Nervous or Shy Candidates

Some candidates may experience nervousness or shyness during interviews, which can impact their ability to present themselves effectively. Employers should aim to create a supportive and encouraging environment to help such candidates feel more at ease.

8.2.1 Establish a Relaxed Atmosphere

Starting the interview with a warm and friendly greeting can help set a positive tone. Employers can begin by introducing themselves, sharing a brief overview of the interview structure, and putting the candidate at ease.

Taking a few minutes for small talk or discussing non-work-related topics can also help candidates relax and feel more comfortable.

8.2.2 Ask Open-Ended Questions

Open-ended questions can encourage nervous or shy candidates to share more about themselves and their experiences. These questions allow candidates to elaborate on their responses and provide greater insights into their qualifications.

For example, instead of asking a closed-ended question like, "Did you work on a team project before?" employers could ask, "Can you tell us about a time when you collaborated with a team to achieve a shared goal?"

Open-ended questions invite candidates to share their stories and experiences in a way that makes them feel more at ease.

8.3 Addressing Salary Expectations

Discussing salary expectations can be challenging for both employers and candidates. However, addressing this topic openly and transparently is crucial to ensure alignment between the candidate's expectations and the company's budget for the role.

8.3.1 Set Expectations Early

During the interview process, it's essential to communicate the salary range or compensation package early on. This approach helps manage candidate expectations and ensures that both parties are on the same page before proceeding with further interviews.

Clearly conveying the salary range can save time and effort for both employers and candidates, preventing potential misalignments later in the hiring process.

8.3.2 Explore Other Forms of Compensation

If a candidate's salary expectations exceed the company's budget, employers can explore other forms of compensation to make the offer more appealing. This may include additional benefits, flexible work arrangements, professional development opportunities, or performance-based incentives.

For example, an employer might say, "While we may not be able to meet your desired salary at this time, we offer competitive benefits and a clear path for career growth within the organization."

By discussing alternative forms of compensation, employers can find solutions that meet both the candidate's expectations and the company's financial constraints.

In conclusion, navigating challenging interview scenarios with professionalism and empathy is essential for creating a positive candidate experience and ensuring fair and inclusive hiring practices. By focusing on candidates' skills and achievements, fostering a relaxed atmosphere, and addressing salary expectations transparently, employers can conduct interviews that leave a lasting positive impression on candidates.

In the next chapter, we will explore the power of feedback in the interview process and how constructive feedback can benefit both employers and candidates. Let's continue on this journey to unlock the full potential of effective interviews for both employers and employees.

Chapter 9: The Power of Feedback in the Interview Process

In Chapter 9, we will explore the significance of feedback in the interview process and its transformative impact on both employers and candidates. Constructive feedback is a valuable tool for improving the interview experience, enhancing candidate engagement, and refining the hiring process. By embracing a culture of feedback, employers can foster growth, strengthen their employer brand, and attract top talent. Let's delve into the various aspects of providing and receiving feedback during the interview journey.

9.1 The Role of Constructive Feedback

Constructive feedback is feedback that is specific, actionable, and focused on areas of improvement. Its purpose is not to criticize but to provide insights that enable candidates and employers to grow and enhance their interview performance.

9.1.1 Feedback for Candidates

Providing candidates with constructive feedback, whether they are successful or not, can be a game-changer in their professional development. Constructive feedback allows candidates to gain a deeper understanding of their strengths and areas for improvement, empowering them to make meaningful adjustments for future opportunities.

For example, if a candidate's interview revealed a need for improved communication skills, the employer could provide feedback such as, "Your technical knowledge was impressive, but we recommend working on providing more concise responses during interviews to highlight your expertise more effectively."

By offering actionable feedback, employers support candidates' growth and demonstrate their commitment to candidates' success.

9.1.2 Feedback for Employers

Feedback in the interview process is not limited to candidates; employers can also benefit from receiving feedback from candidates about their interview experience. This feedback can shed light on the effectiveness of the interview process, the clarity of job descriptions, and the overall candidate experience.

Employers can collect feedback through post-interview surveys, candidate feedback forms, or even informal discussions.

For instance, if multiple candidates express confusion about the job requirements, employers may realize the need to revise and clarify the job description.

9.2 The Art of Giving Constructive Feedback

Providing constructive feedback requires finesse and empathy. Employers should consider the following best practices when delivering feedback to candidates:

9.2.1 Be Specific and Timely

Constructive feedback is most effective when it is specific to the interview and provided promptly. Avoid general statements and provide concrete examples to illustrate areas of improvement.

For instance, instead of saying, "Your presentation skills need improvement," employers can say, "During the presentation segment of the interview, it would be beneficial to maintain better eye contact with the audience for increased engagement."

9.2.2 Emphasize the Positive

When delivering feedback, it's essential to balance areas of improvement with positive reinforcement. Acknowledge the candidate's strengths and achievements to foster a positive atmosphere.

For example, employers might say, "Your problem-solving abilities demonstrated during the case study discussion were impressive. To further enhance your responses, we recommend providing more context before diving into your solutions."

9.2.3 Offer Guidance for Improvement

Incorporate actionable suggestions for improvement in the feedback. Encourage candidates to seek additional resources, training, or coaching to enhance their skills.

For instance, employers could recommend relevant workshops, online courses, or practice sessions to help candidates strengthen specific areas.

9.3 Receiving Feedback Gracefully

Just as employers provide feedback to candidates, they should also be open to receiving feedback from candidates. Creating an environment where candidates feel comfortable providing feedback can improve the overall candidate experience and help employers refine their interview process.

9.3.1 Welcome Feedback

Express openness to receiving feedback from candidates and assure them that their insights are valuable. Candidates may have unique perspectives that can help employers make meaningful improvements.

9.3.2 Act on Feedback

When candidates provide feedback, employers should take it seriously and consider implementing necessary changes. Demonstrating responsiveness to feedback reinforces a culture of continuous improvement.

9.3.3 Use Feedback to Enhance the Interview Process

Collect and analyze feedback systematically to identify patterns or common themes. Use this data to refine the interview process, adjust job descriptions, or improve communication with candidates.

In conclusion, feedback is a powerful tool in the interview process that benefits both employers and candidates. Providing constructive feedback allows candidates to grow professionally and enhances their chances of success in future opportunities. Embracing feedback from candidates enables employers to refine their interview process and create a positive candidate experience, contributing to a strong employer brand.

In the final chapter, we will summarize the key takeaways from this book and emphasize the importance of continuous improvement in the interview process. Let's conclude this journey to unlock the power of effective interviews for both employers and employees.

Chapter 10: Embracing Continuous Improvement in the Interview Process

In Chapter 10, we will explore the importance of continuous improvement in the interview process. The interview landscape is ever-evolving, and embracing a culture of learning and adaptation is vital for employers to stay competitive and attract top talent. By consistently seeking ways to enhance the interview process, employers can create a positive candidate experience, improve hiring outcomes, and foster a workplace culture that values growth and development. Let's delve into the key aspects of continuous improvement in the interview process.

10.1 Learning from Past Experiences

One of the foundations of continuous improvement is learning from past experiences. Employers should regularly review the interview process, analyze candidate feedback, and evaluate hiring outcomes to identify areas for enhancement.

10.1.1 Conduct Post-Interview Reviews

After each interview, interviewers should take the time to review their notes and evaluations. Reflecting on the interview process can help interviewers identify strengths and weaknesses in their approach and identify opportunities for improvement.

For example, interviewers may realize that certain questions consistently generate insightful responses, while others may need refinement to provide better insights into candidates' qualifications.

10.1.2 Seek Candidate Feedback

Actively seek feedback from candidates regarding their interview experience. Providing candidates with the opportunity to share their thoughts and suggestions can yield valuable insights into the effectiveness of the interview process and the candidate's perception of the organization.

Feedback forms, surveys, or follow-up emails are effective ways to gather candid feedback from candidates.

10.1.3 Analyze Hiring Outcomes

Evaluate the outcomes of the hiring process regularly. Assess whether the selected candidates perform well in their roles and align with the organization's culture and values.

By analyzing hiring outcomes, employers can identify any patterns or trends that may indicate areas for improvement in the interview process.

10.2 Embracing Innovation and Technology

The interview process can benefit from innovation and the strategic use of technology. Embracing new tools and techniques can enhance efficiency, streamline candidate assessments, and broaden access to talent.

10.2.1 Explore Innovative Interview Formats

Consider implementing innovative interview formats, such as panel interviews, video assessments, or simulations. These alternative formats can provide a more comprehensive view of candidates' abilities and decision-making skills.

For example, using virtual reality simulations can allow candidates to showcase their problem-solving skills in real-life scenarios related to the job they are applying for.

10.2.2 Leverage AI-Powered Tools

AI-powered tools can significantly impact the interview process, from initial candidate screening to assessment and evaluation. Integrating AI-driven technologies can save time, reduce bias, and help identify top candidates more effectively.

However, it is crucial to ensure that these tools are thoroughly tested and regularly audited to avoid reinforcing biases and to maintain fairness in candidate evaluations.

10.3 Training and Development for Interviewers

Interviewers play a pivotal role in the hiring process. Providing interviewers with the necessary training and development can lead to more effective candidate assessments and a more consistent interview experience.

10.3.1 Conduct Interviewer Training Workshops

Organize regular training workshops for interviewers to enhance their interviewing skills, including active listening, effective questioning, and unbiased evaluation.

Training can also focus on maintaining a positive candidate experience, even for candidates who may not be selected for the role.

10.3.2 Encourage Peer-to-Peer Learning

Facilitate opportunities for interviewers to share their experiences and learn from one another. Peer-to-peer learning can lead to the adoption of best practices and foster a collaborative interview culture.

For instance, interviewers might discuss effective questioning techniques or how to assess soft skills during interviews.

10.4 Building an Employer Brand Focused on Growth

Continuous improvement in the interview process is an integral part of building an employer brand that values growth, development, and a positive candidate experience.

10.4.1 Showcase a Culture of Learning

Communicate the organization's commitment to continuous improvement and learning. Highlight opportunities for career development and growth within the company.

Prospective candidates are more likely to be attracted to organizations that prioritize employee growth and provide a supportive environment for professional development.

10.4.2 Incorporate Feedback into Your Employer Branding

Use feedback from candidates to improve and refine your employer branding. Highlight testimonials and positive experiences shared by candidates to showcase a candidate-centric interview process.

For example, feature candidate testimonials on your career website or share positive feedback on social media platforms.

In conclusion, embracing continuous improvement in the interview process is essential for employers to stay competitive, attract top talent, and maintain a positive employer brand. By learning from past experiences, embracing innovation, training interviewers, and showcasing a culture of growth, employers can create an interview process that sets the stage for successful hiring and fosters a thriving workplace environment.

Thank you for joining us on this journey to explore the power of effective interviews for both employers and employees. Remember, the interview process is a two-way street, offering valuable opportunities for both employers and candidates to find the perfect fit and unlock their full potential together.

Appendix A: Sample Interview Questions

In this appendix, we have compiled a selection of sample interview questions that employers can use to assess candidates' qualifications, skills, and fit for the job. These questions are organized into different categories to cover various aspects of a candidate's experience and personality. Employers can customize these questions to suit their specific needs and the requirements of the position they are hiring for.

General Questions:

- Can you tell us about yourself and your background?
- What interests you the most about this role and our organization?
- How do you handle challenges or difficult situations at work?
- Describe a time when you worked effectively as part of a team.
- How do you stay organized and manage multiple tasks or projects simultaneously?

Skills and Qualifications:

- What relevant experience do you have that makes you a strong fit for this position?
- How do you stay updated with the latest industry trends and developments?
- Can you provide an example of a successful project you led or contributed to?
- Describe your proficiency with [specific software/tool relevant to the position].

- How do you ensure attention to detail in your work?

Problem-Solving and Decision-Making:

- Describe a situation where you had to make a critical decision with limited information.

- How do you approach solving complex problems?

- Can you share an example of when you identified a problem and implemented a successful solution?

- How do you handle disagreements or conflicts within a team?

- What steps do you take to ensure your decisions align with the organization's goals?

Communication and Interpersonal Skills:

- Describe a time when you effectively communicated a complex idea to a non-technical audience.

- How do you adapt your communication style when interacting with different stakeholders?

- Can you share an example of when you resolved a conflict between team members?

- How do you provide constructive feedback to your colleagues or team members?

- How do you approach building relationships with clients or customers?

Leadership and Teamwork:

- Describe a successful project you led from start to finish.

- How do you motivate and inspire your team members?

- Can you share an example of when you delegated tasks effectively?

- How do you approach decision-making within a team setting?

- Describe a challenging team situation and how you helped resolve it.

Cultural Fit and Values:

- What attracted you to our company culture and values?
- How do you approach diversity and inclusivity in the workplace?
- Can you provide an example of how you've contributed to a positive work environment in your previous role?
- How do you handle feedback from colleagues and supervisors?
- What do you consider the most important aspect of being part of a team?

These sample interview questions cover a wide range of topics to help employers assess candidates thoroughly and identify the best fit for their organization. It is essential to complement these questions with active listening and follow-up inquiries to gain deeper insights into each candidate's qualifications and potential contributions to the team.

Appendix B: Interview Evaluation Form

An interview evaluation form is a valuable tool for employers to standardize the assessment process, ensure consistency among interviewers, and make informed hiring decisions. This form allows interviewers to rate candidates' performance based on predetermined criteria and provides a structured framework for evaluating their qualifications, skills, and fit for the job. Below is a sample interview evaluation form that employers can use as a reference and customize according to their specific needs.

Candidate Information:

- Name:
- Position Applied For:
- Interview Date:
- Interviewer(s):

Evaluation Criteria:

A. Skills and Qualifications:

__ Exceptional

__ Strong

__ Adequate

__ Below Expectations

__ Not Applicable / Not Observed

Comments:

B. Problem-Solving and Decision-Making:

__ Exceptional

__ Strong

__ Adequate

__ Below Expectations

__ Not Applicable / Not Observed

Comments:

C. Communication and Interpersonal Skills:

__ Exceptional

__ Strong

__ Adequate

__ Below Expectations

__ Not Applicable / Not Observed

Comments:

D. Leadership and Teamwork:

__ Exceptional

__ Strong

__ Adequate

__ Below Expectations

__ Not Applicable / Not Observed

Comments:

E. Cultural Fit and Values:

__ Exceptional

__ Strong

__ Adequate

__ Below Expectations

__ Not Applicable / Not Observed

Comments:

F. Overall Impression:

__ Highly Recommended

__ Recommended

__ Consideration

__ Not Recommended

Comments:

General Comments:

Interviewer(s) Signature(s):

Notes:

- Each interviewer should independently evaluate the candidate based on the predetermined criteria.

- Interviewers should provide specific comments to support their ratings, highlighting strengths and areas for improvement.

- The overall impression is a collective evaluation based on the combined feedback from all interviewers.

- The form can be customized by adding or removing criteria based on the specific requirements of the position and the organization's priorities.

By using an interview evaluation form, employers can objectively assess candidates, facilitate more productive post-interview discussions, and ensure a fair and consistent hiring process. The form also serves as a valuable record for future reference and decision-making related to candidate selection.

Appendix C: Additional Resources for Further Learning

In this appendix, we have curated a list of additional resources that can help you delve deeper into the topics covered in this book, "The Power of Effective Interviews for Employers and Employees." These resources include books, articles, online courses, and websites that offer valuable insights, best practices, and tools to enhance your understanding and proficiency in conducting effective interviews. Whether you are an employer seeking to optimize your hiring process or an individual looking to improve your interview skills, these resources can be valuable assets in your journey towards success.

Books:

1. "The Interview: An Ethnographic Approach" by Christopher G. Ellison

2. "Great Answers to Tough Interview Questions" by Martin John Yate

3. "Interview Like Yourself... No, Really! Follow Your Strengths and Skills to Get the Job in 2019" by A. P. Carpenter

4. "Hire with Your Head: Using Performance-Based Hiring to Build Great Teams" by Lou Adler

5. "Cracking the Coding Interview: 189 Programming Questions and Solutions" by Gayle Laakmann McDowell

Articles:

1. "The Art of the Interview: Tips and Techniques for Effective Hiring" (Harvard Business Review)

2. "How to Conduct a Job Interview: The Complete Guide" (The Balance Careers)

3. "How to Succeed in Behavioral Interviews" (The Muse)

4. "The Dos and Don'ts of Effective Interviewing" (American Psychological Association)

5. "The Hidden Biases in Interview Questions" (Harvard Business Review)

Online Courses:

1. "Effective Interviewing: Techniques for Hiring, Coaching, and Performance Management" (LinkedIn Learning)

2. "Mastering the Job Interview" (Coursera)

3. "The Interview Process: An In-Depth Guide for Job Seekers" (Udemy)

4. "Interviewing and Making Job Offers" (SHRM eLearning)

Websites and Resources:

1. Glassdoor Interview Reviews - www.glassdoor.com/Interview/index.htm

2. InterviewBuddy - www.interviewbuddy.online

3. The Balance Careers Interview Questions - www.thebalancecareers.com/interview-questions-4161919

4. Interviewing.io - interviewing.io

These additional resources cover a wide range of topics related to interviews, from technical job interviews to behavioral interviews and more. Whether you are an employer or a job seeker, these resources can offer valuable guidance, tips, and strategies to navigate the interview process successfully.

Remember, effective interviews are a continuous learning process, and seeking additional knowledge and insights can significantly impact your interview outcomes. Keep exploring and honing your interview skills to unlock the full potential of effective interviews for both employers and employees. Best of luck on your journey!

About the Author

Dr. Raul Dominguez, is a leading expert in Industrial-Organizational (IO) Psychology, renowned for his work on effective interviews and talent acquisition. He is the author of influential business psychology books, including "The Science of Industrial-Organizational Psychology in the Workplace," "Transforming Toxic Workplaces," and "Leading with Impact: The First 50 Days." With a passion for creating positive work environments, Dr. Dominguez continues to inspire organizations globally through his research, writing, and consulting endeavors.